Sensei Self Development

Mental Health Chronicles Series

Understanding and Practicing Positive Self-Talk

Sensei Paul David

Copyright Page

Sensei Self Development - Understanding and Practicing Positive Self-Talk, by Sensei Paul David

Copyright © 2024

All rights reserved.

978-1-77848-341-7
SSD_Journals_Amazon_PaperbackBook_ Understanding and Practicing Positive Self-Talk

978-1-77848-340-0SSD_Journals_Amazon_eBook _Understanding and Practicing Positive Self-Talk

978-1-77848-457-5
SSD_Journals_Ingram_ Paperback_Understanding and Practicing Positive Self-Talk

This book is not authorized for free distribution copying.

www.senseipublishing.com

@senseipublishing
#senseipublishing

Get/Share Your FREE SSD Mental Health Chronicles at www.senseiselfdevelopment.care

or

CLICK HERE

Check Out The SSD Chronicles Series CLICK HERE

Dedication

To those who courageously take action towards self-improvement - you are helping to evolve the world for generations to come.

- It's a great day to be alive!

If Found Please Contact:

_____

Reward If Found:

_____

MY COMMITMENT

I, _____ commit to writing This Sensei Self Development Journal for at least 10 days in a row, starting: _____

Writing this journal is valuable to me because:

_____
_____
_____
_____
_____
_____

If I finish a minimum of 10 consecutive days of writing in this journal, I will reward myself by:

_____
_____
_____
_____

_____

_____

If I don't finish 10 days of writing this journal, I will promise to:

_____

_____

_____

_____

_____

I will do the following things to ensure that I write in my Sensei Self Development Journal every day:

_____

_____

_____

_____

_____

Get/Share Your FREE All-Ages Mental Health eBook Now at
www.senseiselfdevelopment.com
Or CLICK HERE

senseiselfdevelopment.com

Check Out Another Book In The SSD BOOK SERIES:

senseipublishing.com/SSD_SERIES

CLICK HERE

Join Our Publishing Journey!

If you would like to receive FUTURE FREE BOOKS and get to know us better, please click www.senseipublishing.com and join our newsletter by entering your email address in the pop-up box.

Follow Our Blog: senseipauldavid.ca

Follow/Like/Subscribe: Facebook, Instagram, YouTube: @senseipublishing

Scan the QR Code with your phone or tablet
to follow us on social media: Like / Subscribe / Follow

A Message From The Author:
Sensei Paul David

Dear Reader,

Welcome to the world of mental health journaling – a sacred space for self-reflection, growth, and healing. Within these pages, you hold the power to uplift your spirit, invigorate your mind, and nourish your goals.

In a world that often moves at blink-and-you'll-miss-it speed, it's crucial to make time for self-care and self-discovery.

Anxiety, stress, and emotional turbulence may have clouded your mind, making it difficult to find clarity and peace within. But fear not! Together, we will navigate the labyrinth of emotions, and experiences, helping to simplify the path to mental well-being.

This journal is not merely a bunch of blank pages awaiting your words. It is your compassionate companion, offering solace and understanding during your unique journey. Here, you are free to unburden yourself, celebrate small and large victories, and confront the challenges that may still linger.

Within the sheltered realm of these pages, there is no judgment, no expectation, and no pressure. Your unique experience and perspective hold immeasurable worth, and your voice deserves to be heard. Whether you choose to fill the lines with eloquence or simply scribble fragments of your thoughts, please remember each entry is a valuable contribution to your growth.

In this sacred space, you are challenged to take off the mask we so often wear in the outside world. It is here that you can be raw, vulnerable, and authentic – allowing your true self to be seen and embraced without reservation. By giving yourself permission to explore the depths of your emotions and confront the shadows that may lurk within, you will discover profound insights and find the healing you seek over time.

As you embark on this journaling journey, I encourage you to embrace the process itself rather than fixate solely on the outcome. Remember, it is not about reaching a certain destination or ticking off boxes on a list of accomplishments. Rather, it is about cultivating self-awareness, fostering self-compassion, and nurturing a sense of curiosity about the intricate workings of your intelligently beautiful mind.

In the quiet moments of reflection, let your pen become a bridge between your inner world and the possibilities that lie ahead. Create a sanctuary for your thoughts, fears, triumphs, and dreams. As you pour your heart onto these pages, allow your words to be a living testament to courage, resilience, and an unwavering commitment to your own well-being.

I am honored to be a part of your journey, and I believe in your ability to navigate the twists and turns with grace and resilience. Remember, you are not alone in this – countless others have walked similar paths, faced similar challenges, and emerged stronger and wiser on the other side. You have the power to reclaim all of your untapped joy, cultivate a positive mindset that serves you, and foster a deep sense of self-love and peaceful confident. – And it will take a worth effort and time.

So, open the first page of this journal with hope, curiosity, and an open heart and open mind. Embrace the transformative power of self-reflection, and allow it to guide you towards a life of greater fulfilment and peace. Each journaling session is an opportunity to not only connect with yourself but also to rekindle the light within that sometimes flickers but never extinguishes.

Remember, the pages you are about to fill are not just a record of your journey but also a testament to your strength, resilience, and indomitable spirit. Cherish this space, invest in yourself, and let your words be an ode to the magnificent journey of becoming whole.

With great respect for your decision to evolve,

Paul

MY CONVICTION

Please circle your answers below

I am DECIDING to be patient with myself and this PROCESS each time I journal toward my improved state of mental well-being

YES   NO

"The present moment is filled with joy and happiness. If you are attentive, you will see it."

Thich Nhat Hanh

Introduction

Associative Machine

Imagine you're reading a book and suddenly you come across two words:

"bananas" and "vomit."

Firstly, these words probably make you feel a bit uncomfortable. You might even wrinkle your nose or feel slightly queasy. This reaction is automatic; you didn't decide to feel disgusted, it just happened. Your brain, in a split second, associated 'bananas' with 'vomit'.

This reaction is your brain doing what it does best – making connections. It's like when you smell a certain perfume and suddenly remember someone you haven't thought about in years. Your brain loves to link things together, especially if they have emotional weight.

Now, back to our banana and vomit example. After reading those words, your brain is now on high alert for anything related to sickness or bananas. If someone mentions fruit or illness, you're likely to notice it more because your brain has flagged these topics as important.

This whole process is quick and mostly unconscious. You don't really control it; it just happens. It's your brain's way of making sense of the world, by creating stories and connections, even out of random things.

And the most interesting part? Your body reacts too. If you read about something scary, your heart might race a bit. It's all connected – your thoughts, feelings, and even physical reactions. Your brain doesn't just think in abstract ideas; it uses your whole body to understand and respond to the world.

So, when you read 'bananas' and 'vomit', it wasn't just words on a page. Your brain treated it like a real situation, however briefly, and reacted accordingly.

The above example was given by Daniel Kahneman, a Nobel prize-winning psychologist and economist, in his best-selling book 'Thinking Fast and Slow' which I highly recommend. He illustrates the point that our brain is constantly making associations between different ideas. For instance, as soon as I mention Christman. Your brain will activate ideas such as red, old man, Santa Claus, gifts, kids, Jesus, and so on. You might even think about certain smells or locations or events that you personally associate Christmas with. Maybe a Christmas movie you watched as a child. Or something you ate. When I say you "think", I do not mean you are consciously thinking, or even aware of these thoughts being activated inside your brain.

All of these happen below your level of consciousness, for the most part. For instance, walking past a cemetery, ideas like death, ghosts, incense, gray, tears, etc would get activated without you knowing.

But how do we know that that happens?

We know our brains work this way thanks to various experiments. For example, if you have been given books to read about ocean life and marine animals in the waiting room. Later, when researchers ask you to name a color starting with the letter 'B', you're more likely to say "Blue" instead of other colors like "Brown" or "Black." This happens because your recent thoughts about the ocean prime your mind to associate with the color blue, which is commonly linked to water and the sea.

Priming doesn't just affect how we think; it can also influence our actions and feelings without us being aware of it. In a classic experiment, college students were asked to make sentences using a specific set of words. One group got words often linked with old people, like "bingo," "gray," and "Fragile." Another group received a random mix of words. After this word exercise, the students were told to walk down a hallway. What they didn't know was that the researchers were timing their walk.

Interestingly, the group that worked with the 'older' words walked down the hall noticeably slower than the others. It turned out that just being exposed to these words made them act in a way associated with being older - they were unknowingly influenced to walk more slowly.

In another study, people were asked to walk slowly, and this physical act made them prime to recognize words related to old age. This shows a reciprocal effect – thinking about old age can make you act older, and acting older can make you think about aging.

These experiments demonstrate how our thoughts, actions, and even our physical expressions are interconnected. Holding a pencil in your mouth in a way that forces a smile can make cartoons seem funnier, while a frown-like expression can intensify negative emotions. Even nodding or shaking your head while listening to a message can influence whether you agree or disagree with it.

All these examples highlight how our brain is always making connections, often without our conscious awareness. It's a complex, interconnected system that influences how we think, feel, and act in subtle but powerful ways.

Why is this information important for positive self-talk?

All of these underscore the powerful impact positive thinking and actions in general can have on us. Just as the "bananas and vomit" example from Daniel Kahneman shows how certain words can elicit a visceral reaction, positive stimuli can also significantly influence how we feel and behave.

In the same way that thinking about something unpleasant can trigger a negative response, immersing ourselves in positive thoughts, recalling joyful experiences, or surrounding ourselves with uplifting messages can enhance our mood and affect our actions positively. It's a demonstration of how our internal dialogue and memories can shape our emotional state.

This is why the advice to "Fake it till you make it" or "act calm and kind regardless of how you feel" can be quite effective. By intentionally adopting a positive outlook or behavior, even if it doesn't initially feel genuine, we can start to induce genuine feelings of positivity and calmness. It's a practical application of how positive self-talk and actions can lead to a more positive state of mind, influencing not just our emotions but also our overall well-being.

This might seem like great news, but there is also bad news. The opposite is also true. Any negative stimuli – information, self-talk, event, or gesture – can make you feel negative, behave negatively, and think negatively – each feeding off of each other in a loop. This is the same mechanism that traps people in depression. And given that our mind is more attuned to negative stimuli, naturally the negative stimuli have an advantage.

The good news is that just like poison is used to make an antidote, our mind is itself the antidote to its bad effects.

The antidote is to consciously try to arrange our life, in every facet, towards more positivity to counteract the bias we have towards negativity and possibly tilt the favor towards positivity.

This could be anything: writing gratitude journals, reading uplifting news, looking for silver lining in things, making positive friends, having positive interactions, smiling more, and of course positive self-talk.

Benefits of Positive Self-Talk

Self-Esteem

Self-esteem refers to the overall opinion we have of ourselves and the value we place on ourselves as individuals. It's the subjective sense of personal worth or value that we carry. High self-esteem means that we generally see ourselves positively, recognizing our worth and our right to be happy and successful. Conversely, low self-esteem is characterized by a lack of confidence and feeling unworthy or incapable.

Research has shown a strong link between positive self-talk and self-esteem. For instance, a study published in the Journal of Personality and Social Psychology found that positive self-statements can boost self-esteem and general well-being. Another research, conducted by the University of Texas, suggested that positive self-talk can significantly reduce stress levels and enhance coping skills, which are crucial for maintaining healthy self-esteem.

How does positive self-talk improve self-esteem? It works by challenging and neutralizing the negative perceptions you may have about yourself. For example, instead of thinking, "I always mess things up," you might tell yourself, "Everyone makes mistakes. The important thing is to learn from mistakes." This shift in internal dialogue can gradually transform your self-perception.

When you regularly engage in positive self-talk, you start to internalize these affirmative messages. You begin to believe in your ability to overcome challenges, achieve your goals, and handle life's ups and downs. This belief, in turn, enhances your sense of self-worth.

Curbs Negative Emotion

When we encounter problems or stress, it's common to automatically respond with negative thoughts. These thoughts can amplify feelings like anxiety, anger, or sadness.

Positive self-talk helps to interrupt this pattern, offering a way to manage these emotions more effectively.

Consider a scenario where you're attempting something new, like learning a musical instrument. It's common to encounter moments of frustration or to think "I'll never get this right" when progress feels slow, which can lead to feelings of discouragement or self-doubt.

In such moments, employing positive self-talk is a way to shift these negative emotions. Instead of dwelling on the difficulty, you might say to yourself, "Each practice session is making me better, even if I can't see the progress right now." This change in internal dialogue can significantly alter how you feel about the situation. It helps to view the challenge as a part of the learning process, not a personal failure.

Studies have indicated that individuals who practice positive self-talk tend to experience lower levels of distress when faced with potential stressors. This is because positive self-talk helps to reframe the situation, reducing the emotional weight it carries. It acts as a buffer against the immediate surge of negative emotions, providing a more balanced perspective in challenging situations.

Resilience

Positive self-talk increases one's ability to face and bounce back from difficulties i.e. resilience. When faced with adversity, such as a personal loss or professional failure, individuals often encounter a barrage of negative emotions and thoughts. Without management, these can undermine one's ability to cope and bounce back.

By engaging in positive self-talk, individuals can reframe their perspective on the challenge at hand. Instead of being overwhelmed by thoughts like "I can't get through this," they might tell themselves, "I have overcome challenges before, I can do it again." This kind of self-communication fosters a sense of personal capability and hope, which are critical components of resilience.

Positive self-talk helps maintain a problem-solving outlook even during setbacks, encouraging one to view obstacles as temporary and surmountable. It shifts the focus from what has gone wrong to how one can learn or grow from the experience.

Scientific studies support the role of positive self-talk in enhancing resilience. Individuals who practice positive self-talk tend to experience less stress and more positive emotions during hardships, contributing to quicker recovery and better overall outcomes. This is particularly notable in fields like sports and high-pressure professions, where resilience can significantly affect performance and well-being.

Encourages Risk Taking

Positive self-talk encourages risk-taking by bolstering confidence and reducing the fear of failure. When faced with potential risks, like starting a new venture or trying something out of your comfort zone, negative thought patterns saying "I might fail" or "It's too risky" can be paralyzing. This fear can prevent you from taking the necessary steps.

Positive self-talk changes this mindset. By affirming your abilities and the possibility of success, such as telling yourself, "I have what it takes to succeed," or "Even if it doesn't work out, I'll learn something valuable," you shift your focus from fear of failure to the potential for positive outcomes.

This mindset, backed by research in behavioral psychology, shows that when individuals engage in positive self-talk, they are more likely to take calculated risks. This is because positive self-talk reduces anxiety and fear, making the prospect of taking a risk seem less daunting and more manageable.

By fostering a more courageous and adventurous mindset, positive self-talk can lead you to seize opportunities you might otherwise shy away from. It encourages a proactive approach to life, where taking risks is seen as a necessary step for innovation and personal growth.

Improved Physical Health

Studies in health psychology have found that positive self-talk can influence physical well-being. People who engage in positive self-talk are more likely to stick with exercise regimes and healthy eating plans. Additionally, this positive mindset is linked to lower stress levels, which is beneficial for overall health. Stress can negatively impact various aspects of physical health, from heart health to immune function, so managing stress through positive self-talk can have a ripple effect on your physical well-being.

How to Practice Positive Self-Talk

How To Stay Positive In A Negative Situation

Questions to Ask Yourself

1. Is this worth getting upset over?
2. What is the lesson here? What can I learn from this?
3. Am I overreacting or overthinking the situation?
4. How might someone I admire handle this situation?
5. What strengths do I have that can help me through this?
6. Five years from now, will this matter as much as it does today?
7. What will I wish I had done when I look back on this moment?
8. Is there a way to turn this obstacle into a stepping stone?
9. What would I advise a friend to do in this situation?
10. What part of this situation is within my power to change?

Things to Remind Yourself Under a Negative State of Mind

1. The past cannot be changed.
2. Opinions don't define reality.
3. Journeys differ.
4. Judgments reflect the judger.
5. Overthinking leads to sadness.
6. Happiness is internal.
7. Thoughts influence mood.
8. Smiles spread.
9. Kindness costs nothing.
10. It's okay to move on.
11. What goes around comes around.
12. Time heals everything

S-O-S Method for Halting Negative Self-Talk

Stop: When you notice negative thoughts, mentally tell yourself "Stop!" This pause gives you the chance to catch the thought and break the negative cycle.

Observe: Take a moment to really listen to what you're telling yourself and acknowledge the feelings these thoughts are generating.

Shift: Change your response by employing positive strategies. Replace the negative self-talk with affirmations or focus on constructive solutions to shift your mindset.

Try this Instead...

- Instead of "I'm not good at this," I can ask myself, "What pieces am I not seeing yet?"
- Instead of "I give up," I can motivate myself by thinking, "I'll revisit the strategies I've learned and try again."
- Instead of "This is too hard," I can challenge myself with, "I'll tackle this step by step, and it will take some patience and effort."
- Instead of "I can't make this any better," I can encourage myself with, "Every attempt is a chance to improve, so I'll continue working on it."
- Instead of "I just can't do math," I can shift my mindset to, "I'll focus on improving my math skills a little each day."
- Instead of "I made a mistake," I can see it as, "Every mistake is an opportunity to learn and become better."
- Instead of "She's so smart. I will never be that smart," I can think, "I'll learn how she approaches problems and adapt it to my learning style."

Talk to yourself as if you were talking to...
- Your best friend: "You're doing an amazing job, keep it up!"
- A child: "It's tough, but I believe in you. You can do this."
- A stranger: "Would you like some assistance with that?"
- Your pet: "One more lap around the park, then we'll rest."
- Your love interest: "There's so much about you that I appreciate."

Collect Quotes, Aphorisms, and Sayings that You Can Use

Here's a selection tailored for various circumstances:

For Overcoming Challenges:
- "The gem cannot be polished without friction, nor man perfected without trials."
- Chinese Proverb

When Seeking Courage:

- "Fortune favors the brave."

– Latin Proverb

Embracing Change:

- "Change is the law of life. And those who look only to the past or present are certain to miss the future."
- – John F. Kennedy

For Reflection and Peace:

- "The quieter you become, the more you can hear."
- Ram Dass

Encouraging Persistence:

- "A river cuts through rock, not because of its power, but because of its persistence."
- – James N. Watkins

Spurring Action and Initiative:

- "He who hesitates is lost." – Proverb

Promoting Self-Compassion:

- "Be gentle with yourself. You're doing the best you can." – Unknown

Use Milder Language

Switching to milder language in your self-talk means using words that are less harsh and more forgiving. For instance, if you're not happy with how you handled a situation, instead of thinking, "I'm so stupid," try saying, "I made a mistake, but I can learn from it." This small change in wording can reduce the negative impact on your mood and self-esteem.

Say you're working on a project and it's not going as planned. Thinking "I'm terrible at this" can make you feel defeated. But if you shift to "I'm facing some challenges, but I'm working on them," it can keep you motivated and more open to finding solutions.

Avoiding extreme language like "I always fail" or "I can never do anything right" is also part of using milder language. These absolutes are rarely true and can make any situation feel worse than it is. Changing them to "I sometimes struggle, but I also have successes" offers a more balanced view of yourself and your abilities.

Journaling

Journaling is a powerful tool for positive self-talk. It involves writing down your thoughts and feelings, which can help you process emotions and gain clarity. When you journal, you have the opportunity to reflect on your experiences, notice patterns in your thinking, and consciously shift negative thoughts to more positive ones.

For example, if you're feeling overwhelmed, writing about it in your journal allows you to explore these feelings in depth. You can then challenge any negative thoughts by reframing them in your writing. Instead of journaling "I can't handle this," you might write, "This is challenging, but I have handled tough situations before."

Journaling also serves as a space to celebrate successes and express gratitude, both of which are key components of positive self-talk. Regularly noting things you are grateful for or achievements, no matter how small, can shift your focus from what's going wrong to what's going right.

Over time, the act of journaling can help develop a more positive and supportive internal dialogue. It becomes a practice where you can confront negative thoughts, understand them, and transform them into a narrative that empowers and uplifts you.

Put Things in Perspective

Putting things in perspective is an important aspect of positive self-talk. It involves looking at situations from a broader viewpoint to evaluate their true impact on your life. This practice helps in distinguishing between minor issues and significant problems, reducing unnecessary stress and anxiety.

For example, if you're upset about a mistake at work, putting it in perspective means asking yourself questions like, "Will this matter in a year?" or "What's the worst that could happen, and how likely is that?" This approach can reveal that the mistake, while inconvenient, isn't as catastrophic as it may initially seem.

Use the Phrase "At least I..."

Using the phrase "At least I..." is a simple yet effective way to shift your focus to the positive aspects of a challenging situation. It's a form of self-talk that helps you acknowledge what you have accomplished or what's going well, even in the midst of difficulty.

For instance, if you're disappointed about not getting a promotion, saying to yourself, "At least I gained valuable experience and skills," can change your perspective. This phrase helps you see the value in the experience, despite the outcome not being what you hoped for.

Similarly, if you're feeling down about a social event that didn't go as planned, reminding yourself, "At least I tried something new and stepped out of my comfort zone," can be uplifting. It's a way of recognizing your effort and bravery, which is a positive takeaway regardless of the event's success.

The phrase "At least I..." acts as a tool to counterbalance negative thoughts, encouraging you to recognize and appreciate the positive aspects of any situation. It fosters gratitude and a sense of accomplishment, which are important for maintaining a positive outlook.

– And being funny helps.

Be Reasonable

"Be Reasonable" in self-talk means aligning your expectations with the realities of everyday life, including the likelihood of certain events and the typical time frames things require. It's about acknowledging that life is unpredictable and not everything always goes as planned.

For instance, if you lose a $100 bill, rather than being overly hard on yourself, reasonable self-talk would be, "It's normal for people to occasionally lose or misplace things." This acknowledges that such incidents can and do happen in the normal course of life.

Slip-ups are a part of everyday existence. Say you forget an appointment or a commitment; rather than thinking, "I'm always so forgetful," a more balanced view is, "Everyone forgets things sometimes, especially when busy. I'll find ways to remind myself in the future."

The same thing goes for your weaknesses. You can't expect to not have any weaknesses. Maybe you are not as good at talking to people like others. Or you are in your 20s and still don't know how to drive. That's okay. You have weaknesses, like, what's the number, 7 billion others.

Similarly, when learning something new, like tennis or a new language, being reasonable means recognizing that proficiency takes time. You can't expect to be an expert overnight or even within a few months. Progress in skills, whether it's sports, technology, or social abilities, is gradual and dependent on the time and effort invested.

In essence, adopting a reasonable approach in your self-talk means evaluating your actions and expectations against the backdrop of common life experiences. It's about understanding that mistakes, forgetfulness, and not being skilled at everything are normal aspects of life, not personal failings. This perspective fosters a more forgiving view of yourself, reducing unnecessary stress and self-criticism.

Build a Routine

Building a routine is essential for making positive self-talk a natural part of your daily life. Without a structured approach, it's easy to fall back into negative thinking patterns. Establishing a routine ensures that positivity becomes a habit, something you do regularly without having to consciously decide to do it each time.

Here is a routine you can try:

1. Morning Visualization: Begin your day with a 5-minute visualization exercise. Picture a positive outcome for your day's key events. Imagine yourself succeeding and handling challenges with grace.
2. Afternoon Walk Affirmations: If possible, take a short walk in the afternoon. Use this time to repeat affirmations to yourself, focusing on your strengths and achievements.
3. Evening Gratitude Journal: In the evening, write down three things you were grateful for that day. These could be as simple as enjoying a good meal, having a productive work session, or a pleasant interaction.

4. Bedtime Positive Recap: Before going to bed, spend a few minutes reflecting on the positive aspects of your day. Even on tough days, try to find at least one positive thing to focus on.
5. Weekly Reflection Activity: Once a week, engage in a creative activity like drawing, painting, or writing that reflects your positive experiences or learnings from the week.

By incorporating these steps into your daily and weekly routine, positive self-talk will gradually become an automatic response to everyday situations.

Make Rules

Just like routines, rules provide a clear framework for how to respond in certain situations, making it easier to stick to positive habits. You don't have to overthink every choice when you have clear rules. And you remember them better.

Here are some rules you can try:
1. Only check social media once a day to reduce negative comparisons.
2. Dedicate 10 minutes daily to mindfulness or meditation.

3. Limit self-criticism to constructive feedback only.
4. Replace "I must do everything perfectly" with "It's okay to be good enough."
5. When feeling overwhelmed, take five deep breaths before responding.
6. Allocate a specific time each week for personal reflection and goal setting.
7. If negative self-talk arises, write it down and challenge its validity.
8. Before sleeping, recall one positive action I took during the day.
9. Choose a motivational quote each week to focus on.
10. Turn "I can't" statements into "I can try" or "I can learn."

Creating your own set of rules for different situations can significantly streamline your decision-making process. With these rules in place, you eliminate the need for constant overthinking and can respond more effectively to various scenarios. This approach is more reliable than relying solely on intuition. Consider police officers: those who have clear protocols for different situations are often better equipped to handle high-pressure decisions than those who rely on making split-second decisions without such guidance. Having a predefined set of rules to follow can provide clarity and direction, much like a trained officer in the field.

Before We Get Started...

Remember, mindfulness journaling is a personal practice, and these questions are meant to guide and inspire you. Feel free to adapt and modify them to suit your needs and preferences. Explore, reflect, and embrace the opportunity to deepen your self-awareness and cultivate a sense of inner peace.

Date ___/___/___ : S M T W Th F S

I feel:
(please circle)

because _____ because _____ because _____ because _____ because _____

Today I Am Grateful For
1. _____
2. _____
3. _____

What could help transform today into a remarkable day?

Reflective Writing
How has your understanding of positive self-talk evolved over time?

_____
_____
_____
_____
_____
_____
_____

What is positive self-talk?

a) Negative thoughts and beliefs about oneself
b) Positive thoughts and beliefs about oneself
c) Repeating phrases or mantras in your head
d) Expressing your thoughts and feelings out loud

All Are Correct - Choose The Response You Feel Is Most Important To Remember

Date ___/___/___ : S M T W Th F S

I feel:
(please circle)

😊 because _____
😁 because _____
😌 because _____
😣 because _____
😠 because _____

Today I Am Grateful For
1. _____
2. _____
3. _____

What could help transform today into a remarkable day?

Reflective Writing
In what ways can positive self-talk help you to achieve your goals?

_____
_____
_____
_____
_____
_____
_____

How can positive self-talk benefit you?

a) It can lower your self-esteem
b) It can help you achieve your goals
c) It can increase feelings of self-doubt
d) It can lead to negative self-perception

All Are Correct - Choose The Response You Feel Is Most Important To Remember

Date ___/___/___ : S M T W Th F S

I feel:
(please circle)

because _____ because _____ because _____ because _____ because _____

Today I Am Grateful For
1. _____
2. _____
3. _____

What could help transform today into a remarkable day?

Reflective Writing

What techniques do you find most helpful when it comes to practicing positive self-talk?

_____
_____
_____
_____
_____
_____
_____

Which of the following is an example of positive self-talk?

a) "I'm never going to succeed"
b) "I'm not good enough"
c) "I can do this"
d) "I always make mistakes"

All Are Correct - Choose The Response You Feel Is Most Important To Remember

Date ___/___/___ : S M T W Th F S

I feel:
(please circle)

😊 because _____
😁 because _____
😌 because _____
😟 because _____
😠 because _____

Today I Am Grateful For
1. _____
2. _____
3. _____

What could help transform today into a remarkable day?

Reflective Writing
What are the benefits of challenging negative self-talk?

_____
_____
_____
_____
_____
_____
_____
_____

Why is it important to practice positive self-talk?

a) It can create a more positive mindset
b) It can worsen your mental health
c) It can lead to self-absorption
d) It can make you dependent on others

All Are Correct - Choose The Response You Feel Is Most Important To Remember

Date ___/___/___ : S M T W Th F S

I feel:
(please circle)

😊 because _____
😁 because _____
😊 because _____
😥 because _____
😠 because _____

Today I Am Grateful For
1. _____
2. _____
3. _____

What could help transform today into a remarkable day?
_____

Reflective Writing

How do you create space for positive self-talk in your daily life?

_____
_____
_____
_____
_____
_____
_____

How can you start incorporating positive self-talk into your daily life?

a) Using harsh and critical language towards yourself
b) Limiting self-praise and compliments
c) Recognizing and challenging negative thoughts
d) Surrounding yourself with negative people

All Are Correct - Choose The Response You Feel Is Most Important To Remember

Date ___/___/___: S M T W Th F S

I feel:
(please circle)

because _____ because _____ because _____ because _____ because _____

Today I Am Grateful For

1. _____
2. _____
3. _____

What could help transform today into a remarkable day?

Reflective Writing

What kind of language do you use when talking to yourself?

_____
_____
_____
_____
_____
_____
_____

Which of the following is NOT a common type of negative self-talk?

a) Overgeneralizing
b) Catastrophizing
c) Gratitude
d) Comparing oneself to others

All Are Correct - Choose The Response You Feel Is Most Important To Remember

Date ___/___/___ : S M T W Th F S

I feel:
(please circle)

because because because because because
_____ _____ _____ _____ _____

Today I Am Grateful For
1. _____
2. _____
3. _____

What could help transform today into a remarkable day?

Reflective Writing

How can you practice self-compassion when it comes to positive self-talk?

_____
_____
_____
_____
_____
_____
_____

How can you shift from negative self-talk to positive self-talk?

a) Ignoring your negative thoughts
b) B. Accepting your negative thoughts as facts
c) C. Replacing negative thoughts with positive affirmations
d) D. Suppressing your negative emotions

All Are Correct - Choose The Response You Feel Is Most Important To Remember

Date ___/___/___ : S M T W Th F S

I feel:
(please circle)

because _____ because _____ because _____ because _____ because _____

Today I Am Grateful For
1. _____
2. _____
3. _____

What could help transform today into a remarkable day?

Reflective Writing

How can you use positive self-talk to build your self-confidence?

_____
_____
_____
_____
_____
_____
_____

How can positive self-talk help with stress management?

a) It can increase stress levels
b) It can create a more negative outlook
c) It can provide a sense of control
d) It can lead to avoidance of problems

All Are Correct - Choose The Response You Feel Is Most Important To Remember

Date ___/___/___ : S M T W Th F S

I feel:
(please circle)

because _____ because _____ because _____ because _____ because _____

Today I Am Grateful For
1. _____
2. _____
3. _____

What could help transform today into a remarkable day?
_____

Reflective Writing
How do you ensure that your positive self-talk is motivating and not overly critical?

_____
_____
_____
_____
_____
_____
_____

How can you use positive self-talk to improve your self-confidence?

a) By focusing on your weaknesses
b) By highlighting your mistakes
c) By acknowledging your strengths and achievements
d) By comparing yourself to others

All Are Correct - Choose The Response You Feel Is Most Important To Remember

Date ___/___/___ : S M T W Th F S

I feel:
(please circle)

😊 because _____ 😁 because _____ 😋 because _____ 😢 because _____ 😠 because _____

Today I Am Grateful For
1. _____
2. _____
3. _____

What could help transform today into a remarkable day?

Reflective Writing

What strategies do you use to recognize and counter the negative self-talk that can creep in?

_____
_____
_____
_____
_____
_____
_____

Which of the following should you avoid when practicing positive self-talk?

a) Using compassionate language towards yourself
b) Being overly critical or harsh
c) Using positive affirmations
d) Expressing your feelings openly

All Are Correct - Choose The Response You Feel Is Most Important To Remember

Date ___/___/___ : S M T W Th F S

I feel:
(please circle)

because _____ because _____ because _____ because _____ because _____

Today I Am Grateful For

1. _____
2. _____
3. _____

What could help transform today into a remarkable day?

Reflective Writing

What kind of situations do you find yourself using positive self-talk in the most?

_____
_____
_____
_____
_____
_____
_____
_____

How can negative self-talk impact your relationships?

a) It can improve communication and trust
b) It can create distance and conflict
c) It can strengthen bonds and connections
d) It can promote healthy boundaries

All Are Correct - Choose The Response You Feel Is Most Important To Remember

Date ___/___/___ : S M T W Th F S

I feel:
(please circle)

because _____ because _____ because _____ because _____ because _____

Today I Am Grateful For
1. _____
2. _____
3. _____

What could help transform today into a remarkable day?

Reflective Writing
How can positive self-talk help you to stay grounded in difficult situations?

_____
_____
_____
_____
_____
_____
_____
_____

How can positive self-talk support your mental health?

a) By increasing feelings of self-criticism
b) By promoting negative self-image
c) By encouraging self-care and self-compassion
d) By reinforcing negative thought patterns

All Are Correct - Choose The Response You Feel Is Most Important To Remember

Date ___/___/___: S M T W Th F S

I feel:
(please circle)

😊 because _____
😁 because _____
😋 because _____
😟 because _____
😠 because _____

Today I Am Grateful For
1. _____
2. _____
3. _____

What could help transform today into a remarkable day?

Reflective Writing
How do you recognize when you are engaging in negative self-talk and how do you stop it?

_____
_____
_____
_____
_____
_____
_____
_____

How can positive self-talk help you achieve your goals?

a) By limiting your potential
b) By increasing self-doubt
c) By providing motivation and encouragement
d) By creating a fear of failure

All Are Correct - Choose The Response You Feel Is Most Important To Remember

Date ___/___/___ : S M T W Th F S

I feel:
(please circle)

because _____ because _____ because _____ because _____ because _____

Today I Am Grateful For

1. _____
2. _____
3. _____

What could help transform today into a remarkable day?

Reflective Writing

How has engaging in positive self-talk impacted your relationships?

_____
_____
_____
_____
_____
_____
_____

Which of the following is NOT a helpful technique for practicing positive self-talk?

a) Using positive affirmations
b) Writing down negative thoughts
c) Surrounding yourself with positive and supportive people
d) Creating a gratitude journal

All Are Correct - Choose The Response You Feel Is Most Important To Remember

Date ___/___/___ : S M T W Th F S

I feel:
(please circle)

😊 because _____
😄 because _____
😌 because _____
😟 because _____
😠 because _____

Today I Am Grateful For
1. _____
2. _____
3. _____

What could help transform today into a remarkable day?

Reflective Writing

What advice would you give to someone who is just starting to practice positive self-talk?

_____
_____
_____
_____
_____
_____
_____

How can practicing positive self-talk impact your overall well-being?

a) It can lead to decreased levels of happiness
b) It can improve your physical health
c) It can worsen your mood and emotions
d) It can increase your self-esteem and confidence

All Are Correct - Choose The Response You Feel Is Most Important To Remember

As we reach the final pages of this journey through "Positive Mindset," I want to extend my heartfelt thanks to you. Your commitment to exploring positivity and its transformative power is not only commendable but a testament to your desire for personal growth and a richer, more fulfilling life experience.

Remember, the journey towards a positive mindset is ongoing and ever-evolving. Each day presents new opportunities to apply these principles, to learn, and to grow. I encourage you to revisit these pages whenever you need a reminder of your incredible potential to foster positivity and resilience in the face of life's challenges.

As we part ways, I leave you with a quote that has been a guiding star in my journey: "The greatest discovery of any generation is that a human can alter his life by altering his attitude."

– William James.

Thank you for allowing me to be a part of your journey. May your path be filled with light, hope, and endless possibilities. Farewell, and may you carry the spirit of positivity with you, today and always.

With gratitude and best wishes,

Sensei Paul David

Reflective Writing

The End

As you close the pages of this mindfulness journal, remember that each word you've written is a step on your journey towards self-awareness and inner peace. Embrace the moments of clarity, the revelations, and even the uncertainties you've encountered along the way. Let this journal be a testament to your growth and a reminder that every day offers a new opportunity to be present, to observe, and to appreciate the simple wonders of life. Carry these lessons forward, and may your path be filled with mindful moments and serene reflections. Until we meet again in these pages, be gentle with yourself and stay anchored in the now.

Mindfulness isn't difficult, we just need to remember to do it.

Thank You!

If you found this book helpful, I would be grateful if you would **post an honest review on Amazon** so this book can reach other supportive readers like you!

All you need to do is digitally flip to the back and leave your review. Or visit amazon.com/author/senseipauldavid click the correct book cover and click on the blue link next to the yellow stars that say, "customer reviews."

As always...
It's a great day to be alive!

Get/Share Your FREE SSD Mental Health Chronicles at www.senseiselfdevelopment.care

Check Out The SSD Chronicles Series CLICK HERE

Get/Share Your FREE All-Ages Mental Health eBook Now at
www.senseiselfdevelopment.com
Or CLICK HERE

senseiselfdevelopment.com

Click Another Book In The SSD
BOOK SERIES:
senseipublishing.com/SSD_SERIES
CLICK HERE

Join Our Publishing Journey!

If you would like to receive FREE BOOKS, please visit **www.senseipublishing.com**. Join our newsletter by entering your email address in the pop-up box

Follow Sensei Paul David on Amazon

CLICK THE LOGO BELOW

FREE BONUS!!!
Experience Over 25 FREE Engaging Guided Meditations!

Prized Skills & Practices for Adults & Kids. Help Restore Deep-Sleep, Lower Stress, Improve Posture, Navigate Uncertainty & More.

Download the Free Insight Timer App and click the link below:
http://insig.ht/sensei_paul

About Sensei Publishing

Sensei Publishing commits itself to helping people of all ages transform into better versions of themselves by providing high-quality and research-based self-development books with an emphasis on mental health and guided meditations. Sensei Publishing offers well-written e-books, audiobooks, paperbacks and online courses that simplify complicated but practical topics in line with its mission to inspire people towards positive transformation.

It's a great day to be alive!

About the Author

I create simple & transformative eBooks & Guided Meditations for Adults & Children proven to help navigate uncertainty, solve niche problems & bring families closer together.

I'm a former finance project manager, private pilot, jiu-jitsu instructor, musician & former University of Toronto Fitness Trainer. I prefer a science-based approach to focus on these & other areas in my life to stay humble & hungry to evolve. I hope you enjoy my work and I'd love to hear your feedback.

- It's a great day to be alive!

Sensei Paul David

Scan & Follow/Like/Subscribe: Facebook, Instagram, YouTube: @senseipublishing

Scan using your phone/iPad camera for Social Media
Visit us at www.senseipublishing.com and sign up for our newsletter to learn more about our exciting books and to experience our FREE Guided Meditations for Kids & Adults.

www.ingramcontent.com/pod-product-compliance
Lightning Source LLC
Chambersburg PA
CBHW072118070526
44585CB00016B/1489